Nehemiah was an exile. Years before, his family and many others had been taken prisoner by the king of Babylon and marched away from home to work in a far-off land. When the king of Persia conquered Babylon, some of the people went back home. But Nehemiah was left behind.

Nehemiah worked in the king's palace at Susa. It was his job to serve the king's wine. He was an important man.

Nehemiah often felt very homesick. He remembered the beautiful city of Jerusalem before it was destroyed. How happy his people had been when they lived there together.

One day, Nehemiah's brother and some other men visited him at the palace.

'What is happening at home?' Nehemiah asked. 'Are the people who have gone back building Jerusalem again?'

The men had nothing but bad news for Nehemiah.

'No,' they said. 'The city of Jerusalem is still just a pile of stones. The walls and gates are all broken down.'

So Nehemiah prayed to God.

'You have kept all the promises you made to your people,' Nehemiah said to God.

'We are the ones who have done wrong,' he said sadly. 'That's why we are prisoners here. But please hear my prayer and keep your promise to take us back home.'

When Nehemiah had prayed he went on with his work. He took the wine to the table where the king was waiting.

The king looked at Nehemiah.

'You seem very sad,' he said. 'What is the matter?'

Nehemiah thought he would be punished
for looking sad.

'I am really sorry,' he said, 'but I just
cannot help it. Someone has told me that
Jerusalem is still a pile of stones and
nobody seems to care.'

'What do you want me to do?' asked the king.

'Please let me go back to rebuild the city of Jerusalem,' Nehemiah said.

The king said he would let Nehemiah go.
They talked for a long time about how
long it would take and what Nehemiah
would need for the job.

'God really answered my prayer,'
thought Nehemiah, as he went to bed
that night.

It was a long, dangerous journey for Nehemiah and his men. When at last they saw Jerusalem they were sad.

That night, when it was dark, Nehemiah rode on a donkey right around the city with a few friends.

'What a lot of work there is to do,' they whispered to each other.

The next day Nehemiah spoke to all the
people.

'God has given us this job to do,' said
Nehemiah. 'He will help us to do it well.'

So they divided into groups. Each
group worked on the section of the city
wall which was near their own homes.

The enemies of God's people saw them building Jerusalem again. They started to tease them.

'What do you think you are doing?' they said. 'You'll never build a wall strong enough even to keep a fox out!'

But when they saw the walls growing strong and high they grew really angry.

They tried to think of plans to break down the walls again.

Nehemiah and his men had to watch out for attack all the time. So some of the men built the wall while others stood on guard. Even the builders wore swords.

17

When the city wall and the gates were finished Nehemiah called all the Jews who still lived nearby to come to the city.

He asked Ezra the priest to read to all the people God's special message to them.

When the Israelites heard what God was saying to them they felt full of praise for their wonderful God. They felt sad, too, that they had not always obeyed him.

'At last,' said Nehemiah, 'the city is strong. We can worship God in his temple and ask him to make it special again.'

So all the Israelites went up the steps to the top of the city walls.

They blew trumpets and sang at the tops of their voices as they walked around the city. Everyone outside could hear them praising God.

God had warned his people that if they disobeyed him they would have to leave their homes — and they did. But he had made them a promise, too.

God had said that if they loved him and turned to him for help he would bring them back to Jerusalem. Now they were home again — home in Jerusalem.

As they marched around their new-built city God's people thanked him for keeping his promise.

**The Lion Story Bible** is made up of 52 individual stories for young readers, building up an understanding of the Bible as one story — God's story — a story for all time and all people.

The Old Testament section (numbers 1–30) tells the story of a great nation — God's chosen people, the Israelites — and God's love and care for them through good times and bad. The stories are about people who knew and trusted God. From this nation came one special person, Jesus Christ, sent by God to save all people everywhere.

Nehemiah's story is told in the Old Testament book of Nehemiah. It takes place when the Jews were in exile in far-off Babylonia, under the rule of the kings of Persia.

Nehemiah was a clever man with an important job. But he did not think he had all the answers. He talked things over with God and asked for his advice and help. Then he went into action.

It was because he was that kind of man that God chose him for a very special job. He knew that Nehemiah would not give up, even when problems came thick and fast and enemies tried to stop him. And so the walls of Jerusalem, God's special city, rose again.

The next book in this series, number 30, tells the famous story of *Jonah*.